This collection of Ho[...]
Comfort Shawls is made[...]
Brand® Homespun® yar[...]
soft bulky weight yarn. T[...]
work up quickly so you will be able [...]
make all of them in no time.
These five Shawls make great gifts. They
are perfect for special occasions such as
birthdays or anniversaries. They also make
wonderful "just because" gifts for your
dear friends. Remember people in need
because a shawl will go a long way toward
giving someone the warmth they need.

LEISURE ARTS, INC.
Maumelle, Arkansas

Homespun®
Comfort Shawls

Cuffed Shawl

Finished Size: 29" long x 53" wide (cuff to cuff)
73.5 cm x 135.5 cm)

SHOPPING LIST
Yarn (Bulky Weight)
[6 ounces, 185 yards
(170 grams, 169 meters) per skein]:
☐ 6 skeins

Crochet Hook
☐ Size K (6.5 mm)
    or size needed for gauge

Additional Supplies
☐ Yarn needle
☐ 1½" (38 mm) button
☐ Pins

GAUGE INFORMATION

10 dc and 6 rows = 4" (10 cm)

Gauge Swatch: 4" (10 cm) square

Ch 12.

Row 1: Dc in third ch from hook and in each ch across: 10 dc.

Rows 2-6: Ch 2 (**does not count as a dc**), turn; dc in each dc across. Finish off.

STITCH GUIDE

DOUBLE CROCHET 2 TOGETHER

(abbreviated dc2tog) (uses 2 dc) ★ YO, insert hook in **next** dc, YO and pull up a loop, YO and draw through 2 loops on hook; repeat from ★ once **more**, YO and draw through all 3 loops on hook (**counts as one dc**).

The Body is worked in two separate pieces. Each piece begins at the wrist and is worked to the center back of the garment, increasing stitches on each edge. The two pieces will be sewn together across a portion of the last row, forming the center back seam.

BODY (Make 2)

Ch 32.

Row 1 (Right side)**:** Dc in third ch from hook and in each ch across: 30 dc.

Note: Loop a short piece of yarn around any stitch to mark Row 1 as **right** side.

Rows 2-10 (Increase rows)**:** Ch 2 (**does not count as a dc, now and throughout**), turn; 2 dc in first dc, dc in next dc and in each dc across to last dc, 2 dc in last dc: 48 dc.

Row 11 (Increase row)**:** Ch 2, turn; 2 dc in first dc, dc in next 9 dc, 2 dc in next dc, (dc in next 8 dc, 2 dc in next dc) 3 times, dc in next 9 dc, 2 dc in last dc: 54 dc.

Row 12 (Increase row)**:** Ch 2, turn; 2 dc in first dc, dc in next dc and in each dc across to last dc, 2 dc in last dc: 56 dc.

Row 13 (Increase row)**:** Ch 2, turn; 2 dc in first dc, dc in next 12 dc, 2 dc in next dc, (dc in next 9 dc, 2 dc in next dc) 3 times, dc in next 11 dc, 2 dc in last dc: 62 dc.

7

Row 14 (Increase row)**:** Ch 2, turn; 2 dc in first dc, dc in next dc and in each dc across to last dc, 2 dc in last dc: 64 dc.

Row 15 (Increase row)**:** Work in same manner as Row 13 increasing in first and last dc with 4 more increases evenly spaced between: 70 dc.

Rows 16-34: Repeat Rows 14 and 15, 9 times; then repeat Row 14 once **more**: 144 dc.

At this point the size can be adjusted. Drape the long edge over one shoulder, allowing the beginning row to rest at your wrist. Keep in mind that you will be adding a 3" (7.5 cm) cuff. If the length is satisfactory, finish off. If you would like it longer and wider, continue to add rows in same manner, then finish off.

ASSEMBLY

Place Body pieces with **wrong** side together. Using the placement diagram on page 17 as a guide, pin pieces together across the last row to about 2" (5 cm) before the center.

Note: If you are making the shawl with a textured yarn, it may be easier to sew the seam using a smooth yarn.

Working through **both** loops of **both** pieces, whipstitch Body pieces together *(Fig. 4a, page 46)*, keeping the sewing yarn farily loose.

CUFF

Row 1: With **right** side facing and working in free loops of beginning ch on one side of Body *(Fig. 2, page 45)*, join yarn with slip st in first ch; ch 9, sc in second ch from hook and in each ch across; slip st in next 2 chs on Body: 8 sc.

Row 2: Ch 1, turn; skip first 2 slip sts, sc in Back Loop Only of each sc across *(Fig. 1, page 45)*.

Row 3: Ch 1, turn; sc in Back Loop Only of each sc across; slip st in next 2 chs on Body.

Rows 4-28: Repeat Rows 2 and 3, 12 times; then repeat Row 2 once **more**.

Row 29: Ch 1, turn; sc in Back Loop Only of each sc across; slip st in last ch on Body, finish off.

With **wrong** sides together and beginning at edge of Cuff, whipstitch first and last rows of Cuff together; then whipstitch across end of rows on Body for 3" (7.5 cm) if desired *(Fig. 4b, page 46)*.

HOOD

Row 1: With **right** side facing, count 22 dc from seam and join yarn with dc in same st *(see Joining With Dc, page 44)*; dc in next 21 dc on same Body piece and in next 22 dc on second Body piece: 44 dc.

Rows 2-20: Ch 2, turn; dc in each dc across.

Row 21: Ch 2, turn; dc in first 20 dc, dc2tog twice, dc in next dc and in each dc across: 42 dc.

Row 22: Ch 2, turn; dc in first 19 dc, dc2tog twice, dc in next dc and in each dc across; finish off leaving a long end for sewing Hood seam: 40 dc.

Fold Hood in half with **wrong** side and matching dc on last row; whipstitch top seam.

FRONT BAND

Row 1: With **right** side facing, join yarn with sc in bottom corner of front edge *(see Joining With Sc, page 44)*, sc in each dc across Body; sc evenly across end of rows on Hood; sc in each dc across Body.

Row 2: Ch 1, turn; sc in each sc across.

Place a marker for buttonhole placement in sc 3½" (9 cm) from Hood.

Row 3: Ch 1, turn; sc in each sc across to marked sc, ch 3, skip next 3 sc (**buttonhole made**), sc in each sc across.

Row 4: Ch 1, turn; sc in each sc across working 3 sc in ch-3 sp.

Row 5: Ch 1, turn; sc in each sc across; finish off.

Sew button on opposite front matching buttonhole.

Design by Shelle Hendrix.

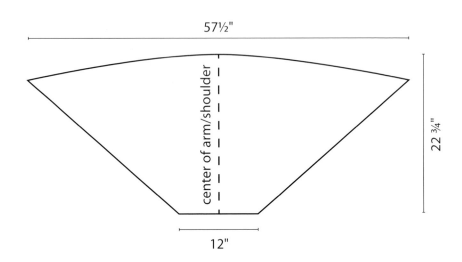

57½"

center of arm/shoulder

22 ¾"

12"

PLACEMENT DIAGRAM

center

center

2"

center back seam

Shrug

SHOPPING LIST

Yarn (Bulky Weight) 🔳 5

[6 ounces, 185 yards
(170 grams, 169 meters) per skein]:

☐ 3{3-4} skeins

Crochet Hook

☐ Size J (6 mm)
or size needed for gauge

Additional Supplies

☐ Yarn needle

SIZE INFORMATION

Finished Size:
   Small{Medium- Large}
Cuff to Cuff Measurement:
   54{56-60}"/137{142-152.5} cm

Size Note: We have printed the instructions for the sizes in different colors to make it easier for you to find:
• Size Small in Blue
• Size Medium in Pink
• Size Large in Green
Instructions in Black apply to all sizes.

GAUGE INFORMATION

In pattern, (ch 1, 3 dc) 3 times =
   4¼" (10.75 cm);
   6 rows = 3¾" (9.5 cm)
Gauge Swatch:
   8½" long x 14" diameter
   (21.5 cm x 35.5 cm)
Work same as Sleeve and Back through Rnd 8.

SLEEVE AND BACK
   (Make 2)
CUFF
Ch 10.

Row 1 (Wrong side)**:** Sc in second ch from hook and in each ch across: 9 sc.

Note: Loop a short piece of yarn around **back** of any stitch on Row 1 to mark **right** side.

Rows 2-17: Ch 1, turn; sc in Back Loop Only of each sc across *(Fig. 1, page 45)*.

Joining Row: Ch 1, turn; with **right** side facing and working in free loops of beginning ch *(Fig. 2, page 45)* **and** in sc on Row 17, slip st in each st across; do **not** finish off.

BODY

Foundation Rnd: Ch 1, working in end of rows on Cuff, work 30 sc evenly spaced around; join with slip st to first sc.

Rnd 1: Ch 4 (counts as first dc plus ch 1, now and throughout), (skip next 2 sc, 3 dc in next sc, ch 1) around to last 2 sc, skip last 2 sc, 2 dc in same st as first dc; join with slip st to first dc: 30 dc and 10 ch-1 sps.

Rnd 2: Ch 1, turn; ★ sc in next dc, ch 1, skip next dc, sc in next ch-1 sp, ch 1, skip next dc; repeat from ★ around; join with slip st to first sc: 20 sc and 20 ch-1 sps.

Rnd 3: Ch 4, turn; ★ skip next sc, 3 dc in next sc, ch 1; repeat from ★ around to last sc, skip last sc, 2 dc in same st as first dc; join with slip st to first dc: 30 dc and 10 ch-1 sps.

Rnds 4-8: Repeat Rnds 2 and 3 twice, then repeat Rnd 2 once **more:** 20 sc and 20 ch-1 sps.

Begin working in rows.

Row 1: Ch 3 (counts as first dc, now and throughout), turn; 2 dc in same st, ★ ch 1, skip next sc, 3 dc in next sc; repeat from ★ across to last sc, leave last sc unworked: 30 dc and 9 ch-1 sps.

Row 2: Ch 1, turn; sc in first 2 dc, ch 1, skip next dc, sc in next ch-1 sp, ch 1, ★ skip next dc, sc in next dc, ch 1, skip next dc, sc in next ch-1 sp, ch 1; repeat from ★ across to last 3 dc, skip next dc, sc in last 2 dc: 21 sc and 18 ch-1 sps.

Row 3: Ch 4, turn; 3 dc in next sc, ch 1, ★ skip next sc, 3 dc in next sc, ch 1; repeat from ★ across to last sc, dc in last sc: 32 dc and 11 ch-1 sps.

Row 4: Ch 1, turn; sc in first dc and in next ch-1 sp, ★ ch 1, skip next dc, sc in next dc, ch 1, skip next dc, sc in next ch-1 sp; repeat from ★ across to last dc, sc in last dc: 23 sc and 20 ch-1 sps.

Row 5: Ch 3, turn; dc in same st, ch 1, ★ skip next sc, 3 dc in next sc, ch 1; repeat from ★ across to last 2 sc, skip next sc, 2 dc in last sc: 34 sc and 11 ch-1 sps.

Row 6: Ch 1, turn; sc in first dc, ch 1, skip next dc, sc in next ch-1 sp, ch 1, ★ skip next dc, sc in next dc, ch 1, skip next dc, sc in next ch-1 sp, ch 1; repeat from ★ across to last 2 dc, skip next dc, sc in last dc: 23 sc and 22 ch-1 sps.

Row 7: Ch 3, turn; 2 dc in first sc, ★ ch 1, skip next sc, 3 dc in next sc; repeat from ★ across: 36 sc and 11 ch-1 sps.

Repeat Rows 2-7 for pattern until piece measures approximately 27{28-30}"/68.5{71-76} cm from edge of Cuff, ending by working Row 3 or 6.

Finish off.

With **wrong** sides together and matching stitches and spaces, whipstitch center back seam *(Fig. 4a, page 46)*.

TASSEL

Cut a piece of cardboard 3" wide x 5" long (7.5 cm x 12.5 cm). Wind a double strand of yarn around the cardboard 7 times. Cut an 18" (45.5 cm) length of yarn and insert it under all of the strands at the top of the cardboard; pull up **tightly** and tie securely. Leave the yarn ends long enough to attach the tassel. Cut the yarn at the opposite end of the cardboard and then remove it *(Fig. A)*. Cut a 16" (40.5 cm) length of yarn and wrap it **tightly** around the tassel twice, ¾" (19 mm) below the top *(Fig. B)*; tie securely. Trim the ends. Knot each end to prevent fraying.

Fig. A	Fig. B
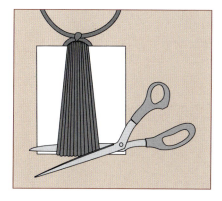	

Attach tassel to top center back point.

Design by Sarah J. Green.

Broomstick Lace Shawl

Finished Size: 23" x 72" (58.5 cm x 183 cm)

SHOPPING LIST

Yarn (Bulky Weight) 🅑5
[6 ounces, 185 yards
(170 grams, 169 meters) per skein]:
☐ 4 skeins

Crochet Hook
☐ Size J (6 mm)
   or size needed for gauge

Additional Supplies
☐ Size 50 broomstick lace pin

GAUGE INFORMATION

In pattern, 7 sts and 4 rows = 3" (7.5 cm)
Gauge Swatch:
   5¼" wide x 3" high
   (13.25 cm x 7.5 cm)
Ch 13.
Work same as Body through Row 4.
Finish off.

BODY

Ch 55.

Row 1: Sc in second ch from hook and in each ch across: 54 sc.

Row 2: Ch 3 (**counts as first dc, now and throughout**), turn; dc in next sc and in each sc across.

Row 3: Ch 1, turn; sc in each dc across.

Row 4 (Broomstick lace)**:** Do **not** turn; slip loop from hook onto pin (*Fig. A*), working from **left** to **right**, skip first sc, ★ insert hook in **next** sc, YO and pull up a loop, slip loop onto pin; repeat from ★ across: 54 loops.

Fig. A

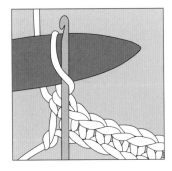

Row 5: Do **not** turn; insert hook from **left** to **right** through first 3 loops on pin *(Fig. B)* and slip these 3 loops off, being careful not to tighten the first loop, YO and draw through all 3 loops on hook, ch 1 *(Fig. C)*, work 3 sc in center of same 3 loops *(Fig. D)*, ★ insert hook from **left** to **right** through next 3 loops on pin, slip these 3 loops off, work 3 sc in center of same 3 loops; repeat from ★ across: 54 sc.

Fig. B

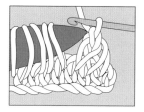

Fig. C

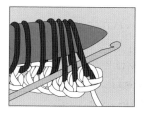

Fig. D

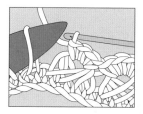

Row 6: Ch 3, turn; dc in next 2 sc and in sp **before** next sc *(Fig. E)*, ★ skip next sc, dc in next 2 sc and in sp **before** next sc; repeat from ★ across to last 3 sc, skip next sc, dc in last 2 sc.

Fig. E

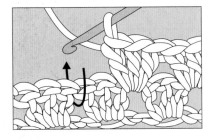

Row 7: Ch 1, turn; sc in each dc across.

Repeat Rows 4-7 for pattern until Shawl measures approximately 72" (183 cm) in length, ending by working Row 7.

Finish off.

Using two strands of yarn, each 16" (40.5 cm) in length, add fringe to short edges of Shawl *(Figs. 5a & b, page 47)*, knotting each end to prevent fraying.

Design by Sarah J. Green.

EASY +

Shell Shawl

Finished Size: 32" x 60"
(81.5 cm x 152.5 cm)

SHOPPING LIST
Yarn (Bulky Weight) BULKY 5
[6 ounces, 185 yards
(170 grams, 169 meters) per skein]:
☐ 3 skeins
Crochet Hook
☐ Size K (6.5 mm)
or size needed for gauge

GAUGE INFORMATION

In pattern,
   9 sts and 5 rows = 4" (10cm)
Gauge Swatch:
   10" wide x 5½" high
   (25.5 cm x 14 cm)
Ch 26.
Work same as Body through
Row 8.
Finish off.

STITCH GUIDE
TREBLE CROCHET
   (abbreviated tr)
YO twice, insert hook in st
indicated, YO and pull up a loop
(4 loops on hook), (YO and draw
through 2 loops in hook) 3 times.

BODY

Ch 74.

Row 1: Sc in second ch from hook,
★ ch 5, skip next 3 chs, sc in next
ch; repeat from ★ across to last
4 chs, ch 2, skip next 3 chs, tr in
last ch: 18 sps.

Row 2 (Right side)**:** Ch 1, turn;
sc in first tr, skip next ch-2 sp,
★ † (2 dc, ch 1, 3 dc, ch 1, 2 dc) in
next ch-5 sp, sc in next ch-5 sp †,
ch 5, sc in next ch-5 sp; repeat
from ★ 4 times **more**, then repeat
from † to † once, ch 2, tr in last sc.

Note: Loop a short piece of yarn
around any stitch to mark Row 2
as **right** side.

Row 3: Ch 1, turn; sc in first tr, ch 5, skip next ch-2 sp, ★ (sc in next ch-1 sp, ch 5) twice, sc in next ch-5 sp, ch 5; repeat from ★ across to last 2 ch-1 sps, sc in next ch-1 sp, ch 5, sc in last ch-1 sp, ch 2, tr in last sc.

Row 4: Ch 1, turn; sc in first tr, ch 5, skip next ch-2 sp, sc in next ch-5 sp, (ch 5, sc in next ch-5 sp) across, ch 2, tr in last sc.

Row 5: Ch 1, turn; sc in first tr, ch 5, skip next ch-2 sp, ★ sc in next ch-5 sp, ch 5, sc in next ch-5 sp, (2 dc, ch 1, 3 dc, ch 1, 2 dc) in next ch-5 sp, sc in next ch-5 sp, ch 5; repeat from ★ across to last ch-5 sp, sc in last ch-5 sp, ch 2, tr in last sc.

Row 6: Ch 1, turn; sc in first tr, ch 5, skip next ch-2 sp, sc in next ch-5 sp, ch 5, (sc in next ch-1 sp, ch 5) twice, ★ (sc in next ch-5 sp, ch 5) twice, (sc in next ch-1 sp, ch 5) twice; repeat from ★ across to last 2 ch-5 sps, sc in next ch-5 sp, ch 5, sc in last ch-5 sp, ch 2, tr in last sc.

Row 7: Repeat Row 4.

Row 8: Ch 1, turn; sc in first tr, skip next ch-2 sp, ★ † (2 dc, ch 1, 3 dc, ch 1, 2 dc) in next ch-5 sp, sc in next ch-5 sp †, ch 5, sc in next ch-5 sp; repeat from ★ 4 times **more**, then repeat from † to † once, ch 2, tr in last sc.

Repeat Rows 3-8 for pattern until Shawl measures approximately 60" (152.5 cm) from beginning ch, ending by working Row 8; do **not** finish off.

EDGING

Ch 1, do **not** turn; sc evenly across end of rows to beginning ch; working in free loops of beginning ch (*Fig. 2, page 45*), 3 sc in same ch as first sc, sc in each ch across to last ch, 3 sc in last ch; sc evenly across end of rows to last row, sc in each st and in each ch across; join with slip st to first sc, finish off.

Design by Sarah J. Green.

Motif Shawl

Finished Size: 25½" x 76½" (65 cm x 194.5 cm)

SHOPPING LIST

Yarn (Bulky Weight) 🅕5
[6 ounces, 185 yards
(170 grams, 169 meters)
per skein]:
☐ 4 skeins

Crochet Hook
☐ Size K (6.5 mm)
 or size needed for gauge

GAUGE INFORMATION

Gauge Swatch: 8½" (21.5 cm) from point to point

Work same as First Motif.

STITCH GUIDE

2-DC CLUSTER (uses one sp)

★ YO, insert hook in sp indicated, YO and pull up a loop, YO and draw through 2 loops in hook; repeat from ★ once **more**, YO and draw through all 3 loops on hook.

3-DC CLUSTER (uses one sp)

★ YO, insert hook in sp indicated, YO and pull up a loop, YO and draw through 2 loops in hook; repeat from ★ 2 times **more**, YO and draw through all 4 loops on hook.

FIRST MOTIF

Ch 8; join with slip st to form a ring.

Rnd 1 (Right side)**:** Ch 2, work 2-dc Cluster in ring, (ch 3, work 3-dc Cluster in ring) 7 times, ch 1, hdc in first 2-dc Cluster to form last ch-3 sp: 8 ch-3 sps.

Note: Loop a short piece of yarn around any stitch to mark Rnd 1 as **right** side.

Rnd 2: Ch 1, 4 sc in last ch-3 sp made, 7 sc in next ch-3 sp and in each ch-3 sp around, 3 sc in same sp as first sc; join with slip st to first sc: 56 sc.

Rnd 3: Ch 1, sc in same st as joining, ch 5, skip next 6 sc, ★ sc in next sc, ch 5, skip next 6 sc; repeat from ★ around; join with slip st to first sc: 8 ch-5 sps.

Rnd 4: Ch 1, (sc, ch 3, sc) in same st (corner sp made), 7 sc in next ch-5 sp, ★ (sc, ch 3, sc) in next sc (corner sp made), 7 sc in next ch-5 sp; repeat from ★ around; join with slip st to first sc: 72 sc and 8 ch-3 sps.

Rnd 5: Slip st in next ch-3 sp, ch 1, (sc, ch 3) twice in same sp, skip next 4 sc, sc in next sc, ch 3, ★ (sc, ch 3) twice in next ch-3 sp, skip next 4 sc, sc in next sc, ch 3; repeat from ★ around; join with slip st to first sc, finish off: 24 ch-3 sps and 24 sc.

26 ADDITIONAL MOTIFS

Work same as First Motif thru Rnd 4; do **not** finish off: 72 sc and 8 ch-3 sps.

Rnd 5 (Joining rnd)**:** Work One Side or Two Side Joining as needed to form 3 strips of 9 Motifs each.

ONE SIDE JOINING

Rnd 5 (Joining rnd)**:** Slip st in next ch-3 sp, ch 1, (sc, ch 3) twice in same sp, skip next 4 sc, sc in next sc, ch 3, ★ (sc, ch 3) twice in next ch-3 sp, skip next 4 sc, sc in next sc, ch 3; repeat from ★ 4 times **more**, sc in next ch-3 sp, ch 1, with **wrong** sides together, slip st in corresponding ch-3 sp on **previous** Motif, ch 1, sc in same sp on **new Motif**, ch 3, skip next 4 sc, sc in next sc, ch 3, working in sc just made **and** in corresponding sc on **previous Motif**, slip st through **both** thicknesses (Picot made), ch 3, sc in next ch-3 sp on **new Motif**, ch 1, slip st in corresponding ch-3 sp on **previous Motif**, ch 1, sc in same sp on **new Motif**, ch 3, skip next 4 sc, sc in next sc, ch 3; join with slip st to first sc, finish off.

TWO SIDE JOINING

Rnd 5 (Joining rnd)**:** Slip st in next ch-3 sp, ch 1, (sc, ch 3) twice in same sp, skip next 4 sc, sc in next sc, ch 3, ★ (sc, ch 3) twice in next ch-3 sp, skip next 4 sc, sc in next sc, ch 3; repeat from ★ 2 times **more**, sc in next ch-3 sp, ch 1, with **wrong** sides together, slip st in corresponding ch-3 sp on **previous Motif**, † ch 1, sc in same sp on **new Motif**, ch 3, skip next 4 sc, sc in next sc, ch 3, working in sc just made **and** in corresponding sc on **previous Motif**, slip st through **both** thicknesses (Picot made), ch 3, sc in next ch-3 sp on **new Motif**, ch 1, slip st in corresponding ch-3 sp on **previous Motif**, ch 1, sc in same sp on **new Motif**, ch 3, skip next 4 sc, sc in next sc, ch 3 †, sc in next ch-3 sp, ch 1, slip st in corresponding ch-3 sp on **adjacent Motif**, repeat from † to † once; join with slip st to first sc, finish off.

Design by Sarah J. Green.

■■□□ **EASY +**

Striped Shawl

Finished Size: 17¾" x 72¼" (45 cm x 183.5 cm)

SHOPPING LIST
Yarn (Bulky Weight) ⑤
[6 ounces, 185 yards
(170 grams, 169 meters) per skein]:

☐ Blue - 3 skeins
☐ Dark Blue - 2 skeins

Crochet Hook
☐ Size K (6.5 mm)
   or size needed for gauge

GAUGE INFORMATION

In pattern,

    10 sts and 6 rows =

    4¼" (10.75 cm)

Gauge Swatch:

    8½" wide x 4¼" high

    (21.5 cm x 10.75 cm)

With Blue, ch 22.

Work same as Body through Row 6.

Finish off.

STITCH GUIDE

TREBLE CROCHET

(abbreviated tr)

YO twice, insert hook in sp indicated, YO and pull up a loop (4 loops on hook), (YO and draw through 2 loops in hook) 3 times.

Each row is worked across the length of the Shawl. When joining yarn and finishing off, leave a 9" (23 cm) length to be worked into fringe.

BODY

With Blue and leaving a 9" (23 cm) end, ch 172.

Row 1 (Right side)**:** Dc in fourth ch from hook **(3 skipped chs count as first dc)**, ★ ch 1, skip next ch, dc in next 2 chs; repeat from ★ across: 114 dc and 56 ch-1 sps.

Note: Loop a short piece of yarn around any stitch to mark Row 1 as **right** side.

Row 2: Ch 3 **(counts as first dc, now and throughout)**, turn; dc in next dc, (ch 1, dc in next 2 dc) across; finish off.

Row 3: With **right** side facing, join Dark Blue with dc in first dc *(see Joining With Dc, page 44)*; dc in next dc, ★ working in **front** of next ch *(Fig. 3, page 45)*, tr in ch-1 sp one row **below**, dc in next 2 dc; repeat from ★ across; finish off: 170 sts.

Row 4: With **wrong** side facing, join Blue with dc in first dc; dc in next dc, ★ ch 1, skip next tr, dc in next 2 dc; repeat from ★ across: 114 dc and 56 ch-1 sps.

Row 5: Ch 3, turn; dc in next dc, (ch 1, dc in next 2 dc) across; finish off.

Row 6: With **wrong** side facing, join Dark Blue with dc in first dc; dc in next dc, ★ working **behind** next ch *(Fig. 3, page 45)*, tr in ch-1 sp one row **below**, dc in next 2 dc; repeat from ★ across; finish off: 170 sts.

Row 7: With **right** side facing, join Blue with dc in first dc; dc in next dc, ★ ch 1, skip next tr, dc in next 2 dc; repeat from ★ across: 114 dc and 56 ch-1 sps.

Rows 8-25: Repeat Rows 2-7, 3 times.

Finish off.

Using one strand of corresponding color yarn, 19" (48.5 cm) in length, add additional fringe to short edges of Shawl *(Figs. 5c & d, page 47)*, knotting each end to prevent fraying.

Design by Sarah J. Green.

General Instructions

ABBREVIATIONS

ch(s)	chain(s)
cm	centimeters
dc	double crochet(s)
dc2tog	double crochet 2 together
hdc	half double crochet(s)
mm	millimeters
Rnd(s)	Round(s)
sc	single crochet(s)
sp(s)	space(s)
st(s)	stitch(es)
tr	treble crochet(s)
YO	yarn over

SYMBOLS & TERMS

★ — work instructions following ★ as many **more** times as indicated in addition to the first time.

† to † — work all instructions from first † to second † **as many** times as specified.

( ) or [ ] — work enclosed instructions **as many** times as specified by the number immediately following **or** work all enclosed instructions in the stitch or space indicated **or** contains explanatory remarks.

colon (:) — the number(s) given after a colon at the end of a row or round denote(s) the number of stitches you should have on that row or round.

GAUGE

Exact gauge is **essential** for proper size. Before beginning your project, make the sample swatch given in the individual instructions in the yarn and hook specified. After completing the swatch, measure it, counting your stitches and rows carefully. If your swatch is larger or smaller than specified, **make another, changing hook size to get the correct gauge.** Keep trying until you find the size hook that will give you the specified gauge.

JOINING WITH SC

When instructed to join with sc, begin with a slip knot on hook. Insert hook in stitch or space indicated, YO and pull up a loop, YO and draw through both loops on hook.

JOINING WITH DC

When instructed to join with dc, begin with a slip knot on hook. YO, holding loop on hook, insert hook in stitch or space indicated, YO and pull up a loop (3 loops on hook), (YO and draw through 2 loops on hook) twice.

Yarn Weight Symbol & Names	LACE ⓪	SUPER FINE ①	FINE ②	LIGHT ③	MEDIUM ④	BULKY ⑤	SUPER BULKY ⑥	JUMBO ⑦
Type of Yarns in Category	Fingering, size 10 crochet thread	Sock, Fingering, Baby	Sport, Baby	DK, Light Worsted	Worsted, Afghan, Aran	Chunky, Craft, Rug	Super Bulky, Roving	Jumbo, Roving
Crochet Gauge* Ranges in Single Crochet to 4" (10 cm)	32-42 sts**	21-32 sts	16-20 sts	12-17 sts	11-14 sts	8-11 sts	6-9 sts	5 sts and fewer
Advised Hook Size Range	Steel*** 6 to 8, Regular hook B-1	B-1 to E-4	E-4 to 7	7 to I-9	I-9 to K-10½	K-10½ to M/N-13	M/N-13 to Q	Q and larger

*GUIDELINES ONLY: The chart above reflects the most commonly used gauges and hook sizes for specific yarn categories.

** Lace weight yarns are usually crocheted with larger hooks to create lacy openwork patterns. Accordingly, a gauge range is difficult to determine. Always follow the gauge stated in your pattern.

*** Steel crochet hooks are sized differently from regular hooks–the higher the number, the smaller the hook, which is the reverse of regular hook sizing.

BACK LOOPS ONLY

Work only in loop(s) indicated by arrow *(Fig. 1)*.

FREE LOOPS OF A CHAIN

When instructed to work in free loops of a chain, work in loop indicated by arrow *(Fig. 2)*.

Fig. 1

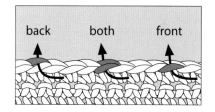

back   both   front

Fig. 2

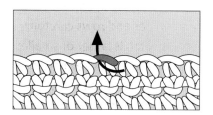

CROCHET TERMINOLOGY		
UNITED STATES		INTERNATIONAL
slip stitch (slip st)	=	single crochet (sc)
single crochet (sc)	=	double crochet (dc)
half double crochet (hdc)	=	half treble crochet (htr)
double crochet (dc)	=	treble crochet (tr)
treble crochet (tr)	=	double treble crochet (dtr)
double treble crochet (dtr)	=	triple treble crochet (ttr)
triple treble crochet (tr tr)	=	quadruple treble crochet (qtr)
skip	=	miss

CROCHET HOOKS																	
U.S.	B-1	C-2	D-3	E-4	F-5	G-6	7	H-8	I-9	J-10	K-10½	L-11	M/N-13	N/P-15	P/Q	Q	S
Metric - mm	2.25	2.75	3.25	3.5	3.75	4	4.5	5	5.5	6	6.5	8	9	10	15	16	19

■□□□ **BEGINNER**	Projects for first-time crocheters using basic stitches. Minimal shaping.
■■□□ **EASY**	Projects using yarn with basic stitches, repetitive stitch patterns, simple color changes, and simple shaping and finishing.
■■■□ **INTERMEDIATE**	Projects using a variety of techniques, such as basic lace patterns or color patterns, mid-level shaping and finishing.
■■■■ **EXPERIENCED**	Projects with intricate stitch patterns, techniques and dimension, such as non-repeating patterns, multi-color techniques, fine threads, small hooks, detailed shaping and refined finishing.

WORKING IN FRONT OF, AROUND, OR BEHIND A STITCH

Work in stitch or space indicated, inserting hook in direction of arrow *(Fig. 3)*.

Fig. 3

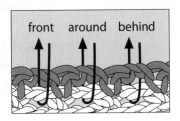

front   around   behind

WHIPSTITCH

Place two pieces with **wrong** sides together. Sew through both pieces once to secure the beginning of the seam, leaving an ample yarn end to weave in later. Insert the needle from **front** to **back** through **both** loops on **both** pieces *(Fig. 4a)*, or in end of rows *(Fig. 4b)*. Bring the needle around and insert it from **front** to **back** through the next loops of both pieces. Continue in this manner across to corner, keeping the sewing yarn fairly loose.

Fig. 4a

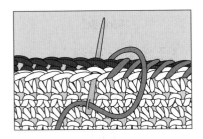

Fig. 4b

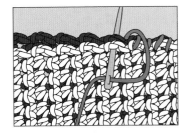

FRINGE

Cut a piece of cardboard 8" (20.5 cm) wide and half as long as specified in individual instructions for strands. Wind the yarn **loosely** and **evenly** around the cardboard lengthwise until the card is filled, then cut across one end; repeat as needed.

Hold together as many strands as specified in individual instructions; fold in half.

With **wrong** side facing and using crochet hook, draw the folded end up through a stitch or space and pull the loose ends through the folded end *(Figs. 5a & c)*; draw the knot up **tightly** *(Figs. 5b & d)*. Repeat, spacing as specified in individual instructions.

Lay flat on a hard surface and trim the ends.

Fig. 5a

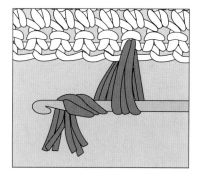

Fig. 5b

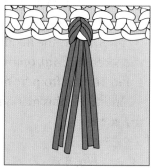

Fig. 5c

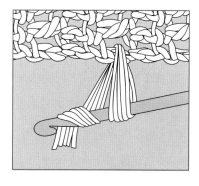

Fig. 5d

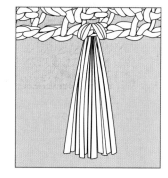

Yarn Information

The items in this book were made using Lion Brand® Homespun® yarn. Any brand of Bulky Weight Yarn may be used. It is best to refer to the yardage/meters when determining how many balls or skeins to purchase. Remember, to arrive at the finished size, it is the GAUGE/TENSION that is important, not the brand of yarn.

For your convenience, listed below are the colors used to create our photography models. Because yarn manufacturers make frequent changes in their product lines, you may sometimes find it necessary to use a substitute yarn or to search for the discontinued product at alternate suppliers (locally or online).

CUFFED SHAWL
#302 Colonial

SHELL SHAWL
#322 Baroque

SHRUG
#345 Corinthian

MOTIF SHAWL
#600 Clouds

BROOMSTICK LACE SHAWL
#315 Tudor

STRIPED SHAWL
Blue - #341 Windsor
Dark Blue - #302 Colonial

Production Team: Instructional/Technical Writer - Lois J. Long; Senior Graphic Artist - Lora Puls; Graphic Artist - Victoria Temple; Photo Stylist - Lori Wenger; and Photographer - Jason Masters.

Motif Shawl made and instructions tested by Janet Akins.